Grace & Peace

God's message for yearning hearts

Grace and Peace — God's message for yearning hearts

Copyright © 2023 by VineSWFL.church | www.vineswfl.church
All rights reserved.

ISBN: 9798853237124
Imprint: Independently published

Cover: Lucas A. N. Fernandes (lucasanfernandes1@gmail.com)
Support writer: Trenton A. Tombs (instagram.com/trentontombs)

Scripture quotations, unless otherwise indicated, are from the (ESV) ® Bible (The Holy Bible, English Standard Version®), copyright © 2001 by Crossway, a publishing ministry of Good News Publishers. All rights reserved. The author has added italics to Scripture quotations for emphasis.

Scripture quotations marked (AMP) are taken from Amplified Bible(R) Copyright (c) 1954, 1958, 1962, 1964, 1965, 1987 by. The Lockman Foundation, La Habra, CA 90631.

When identified Scripture quotations are taken from the Holy Bible, New Living Translation will be followed by (NLT). All rights reserved.

Scripture taken from the New King James Version® will be followed by (NKJV). Copyright © 1982 by Thomas Nelson. Used by permission. All rights reserved.

Any references to historical events, real people, or real places are used fictitiously. Names, characters, and places are products of the author's imagination.

Grace | Peace | Gospel | Evangelism | Discipleship |Vine Church | LifeGroup | Small Groups

CONTENTS

Introduction   5

   1. The God of Grace   7

   2. Grace and Truth   17

   3. Grace, not Religion   27

   4. From Darkness to Grace   37

   5. Time for Grace   45

Appendix. Steps of Grace   53

INTRODUCTION

The combination of grace and peace is an inseparable pair for those who follow, by faith, Jesus. Grace means that will God blesses the one that does not deserve it. It is Jesus saving the one that is still hostile to Him. Grace is the Spirit moving a person's heart for a new life. There is no better place to be than in the grace of God. This means relying on God's unearned favor, having His friendship, presence, resources, and gifts. Amazing grace is amazing because it brings us close to our all-loving God. Only the one that receives grace can have peace with God. Fear, anxiety, and stress are all symptoms of someone that are not at peace with God. Fear of death is evidence that one is not at peace with God. Think about it. If you are unsure of what comes next after you permanently close your eyes, there is only an expectation of judgment. But if I tell you that you can have a complete sense of peace with God by reading this book and trusting its message. Once you have that, everything in your life will be changed. This book is in your hands to give you the perfect divine blessing combination. His grace and His peace. Therefore, I greet you as the Bible teaches, "Grace to you and peace from God our Father and the Lord Jesus Christ."

1.
THE GOD OF GRACE

God so loved you that he took all the limitations out of your way to perceive and receive that love. On God's side, He made everything possible to reach out to your heart. He displayed His love through the creation all around you. Just look deeper, and you will see God's invisible attributes. "His eternal power and divine nature have been clearly perceived" through nature everywhere around you. (Read Romans 1:20).

Today, most renowned scientists discarded the concept that science and faith are conflicting in opposition.[1] Creation points to a creator. As a personal God, His is not distant and oblivious to His people. He cares for you and me. Theologians, philosophers and scientists are all realizing there is a God intentionally showing His grace everywhere. But what is your idea of grace? What do you think of God's plan to save us? Do you still think it is an antiscientific Bronze Age superstition? There is so much evidence of God's order and beauty everywhere that it is hard to deny the designer's existence behind all that design. You may need much more faith to believe in an

---

1 Guillen, Michael. *Believing Is Seeing: A Physicist Explains How Science Shattered His Atheism and Revealed the Necessity of Faith*. Kindle ed. Carol Stream, IL: Tyndale House Publishers, 2021, 35.

atheistic universe than a follower of Christ.[2]

An ordered universe that follows physics laws presupposes a Lawgiver outside this universe. All that is because the all-mighty creator wants us to believe in Him to enjoy His loving presence (Read Hebrews 11:6). You may ask, "Is not God all-powerful? Why does He not do something about people not believing in Him?" God is also all-loving. A premise of love establishes that we must choose to accept (or not) that expression of love. If there is no chance of rejection of God's declaration of love, it is not real love.

What is the ultimate expression of God's love for us?

> *"For God so loved the world, that he gave his only Son, that whoever believes in him should not perish but have eternal life. For God did not send his Son into the world to condemn the world, but in order that the world might be saved through him. (John 3:16-17).*

A Problem

We are in a condition of blindness and deafness to see and perceive God's love. Mankind has sinned and is incapable of perceiving God's plan for them. (Read Romans 3:23). And to make it worst, over the years, I've realized that most people treat sin, particularly their own, like a minor traffic violation. We may rationalize our wrongdoing by telling ourselves, "Yes, of course, sin is breaking God's law, but there are worse criminals out there than me. Besides, no one was wounded, and I have no problem paying the ticket."[3] People think that sin is not a big deal. Is it?

---

[2] Geisler, Norman L. and Frank Turek. *I Don't Have Enough Faith to Be an Atheist*. Kindle ed. Wheaton, IL: Crossway Books, 2021, 389.

[3] Gilbert, Gregory D. *What Is the Gospel?* Kindle ed. Wheaton, IL: Crossway, 2010, 49.

The problem is with God's authority and right to command those to whom He gave life. Sin is a rebellion of the creature against His Creator. God made man and woman in His image and likeness. We were meant to be like Him in a satisfying relationship with Him, displaying His glory to the world. God had a purpose for humans to enjoy. They were to rule His world under Him (Genesis 1:28).

However, they were only the stewards. God is the King. When a restriction was established, "Don't eat the fruit." God reminded us who was still in charge of everything. Therefore, their disobedience was a rejection of God's authority over them. It was deliberate autonomy from Him. Adam and Eve wanted to be, as the Serpent promised them, "like God," so both seized on what they thought was an opportunity to shed the vice-regency and take the crown itself. In all the universe, there was only one thing God had not placed under Adam's feet—God Himself.

Isn't that the same problem today? Parents suffer with their rebellious children because they think love is to receive everything they want. However, parents know best. Giving a 12 oz. piece of chocolate cake before bed is not the best expression of love to a grade-age child. When one is blind to see the love of the Father, instead of feeling protected and cared for, they react with rebellion, denial and distance.

God's love is expressed in His creation. Jesus expresses God's love on the cross. God's love is expressed to you with this message. Are you willing to believe this truth? "Unless you're willing to believe that something might be true, you'll never bother to investigate and see for yourself whether it is true (or not). You'll remain in a state of confident ignorance."[4]

---
[4] Guillen *Believing Is Seeing*, 39.

The consequences of Adam and Eve's sin were disastrous for them, their descendants, and the rest of creation. When they severed ties with God, human hearts shrank, and their minds became preoccupied with self-centered concerns. Humanity is blind to the glory of God, and their souls withered. I understand that for some, the idea that humans are inherently sinful and rebellious is not just scandalous but also offensive to the prideful nature of human hearts. Absolutely repulsive. But that is the truth. That's why it is so absolutely crucial that we understand both the nature and the depth of our sin. Unless a patient is entirely convinced of his terminal state, he will never appropriately accept the treatment. That is what happens with those who deny their sinful condition and still try to fix themselves without the providence medicine of God's love, which is faith in God's forgiveness through the sacrifice of Jesus.

As much as Jesus came to save humanity from an innate sense of guilt, meaninglessness, purposelessness, or emptiness, the issue is more significant than that. Of course, those things are problems, and many people deeply feel them. But the Bible teaches that humanity's fundamental problem—the thing from which we need to be saved—is not meaninglessness or disintegration in our lives or even a debilitating sense of guilt.

If by "sins" we mean "isolated mistakes," then it is not sufficient to declare that Jesus came to free us from sins. The good news means to be rescued from our entire evil nature. One can only accept the good news if they first understand we are actually "dead in our trespasses and sins." (Ephesians 2:1, 5). That is why Jesus was also called the Lamb of God, that takes away the sin of the world (John 1:29). The innocent Lamb's life was sacrificed so we could be saved.

We are not victims of society or our family upbringing. The fact is we are all criminals, unrighteous and deserving of judgment, and until justice is served, there is no way out. Sin is the breaking of a relationship with God. It's not just adultery. It is also rebellion. Not just betrayal but also treason.

God's Righteous Judgment Against Sin

We all will one day stand before God and have no explanation, plea, excuse, or case. That is to be "held accountable to God." The Bible says,

> "[...] every mouth may be stopped, and the whole world may be held accountable to God.?" (Romans 3:19).

The righteous and holy God will not excuse sin. But what will it mean for God to deal with sin, to judge it and punish it? Romans 6:23 says, "The wages of sin is death." Our sin deserves death. That's not just physical death. It is spiritual death, a forceful separating of our sinful, wretched selves from the presence of the righteous and holy God. Our iniquities have made a separation between us and God. (Isaiah 59:2).

It is not just a passive, quiet absence of God. It's more than that. It is God's active judgment against sin; the Bible says it will be terrifying. The final destiny for unrepentant, unbelieving sinners is a place of eternal, conscious torment called "hell." The Bible describes it as a "lake of fire and sulfur," and Jesus says it is a place of "unquenchable fire" (Revelation 20:10; Mark 9:43). For the creature meant to exist in the presence of God, His absence is like a fish out of water. It is suffocating and drowning at the same time. Intolerable.

I understand your discomfort with that reality. We must talk about hell because it is real. We realize that people we love are in danger of spending eternity there. This is the sobering verdict for every person. There is not one of us righteous, not even one.

But...

The Forgiveness on the Cross

In His sacrifice, Jesus said His last words while on the cross. Some say that the last words of a person are very important. The Bible shows us what Jesus uttered.

> *[...] Jesus said, "Father, forgive them, for they know not what they do." [...] (Luke 23:34)*

Three crosses loom on the horizon. In the middle is the Lord Jesus, on the right side a thief, and on the left side another thief. Jesus died the way He always lived. He came to seek sinners, criminals, like us all. He lived to reach them, forgive them, and transform them. And when it was time to die, He died crucified among them. And at the hour of his death, he speaks: "Father, forgive them, for they know not what they do."

A crown of thorns pierced His face, but it did not prevent Him from seeing His Father's love. His hands were nailed to a cross, they could no longer heal people, but He still could pray for us. His feet could no longer walk to reach the sinner, but that didn't stop Jesus from praying for us. His disciples had abandoned Him, and He could no longer teach them, but that didn't stop Jesus from praying for us.

When difficulties arise in life, when we lose our job or our child falls ill, the first thought that assails our mind is that maybe God has abandoned us. The key here is prayer. If Jesus prayed, we also must learn to pray. Above us all exist a God, a Father who always listens to our prayer.

Jesus prayed not for His friends or family. He does pray for His enemies. He prayed for the one that slapped Him, nailed His hands, and spit on His face. He asks the Father to forgive them. On the cross, while suffering, with every drop of blood taking His life, Jesus releases forgiveness. His forgiveness is God's forgiveness. Justice was served, and now, forgiveness is available.

In love, God is calling you to be back home. Your original place of purpose. He planned amazing things for you as a son. Through Jesus Christ, God is satisfied. Because of that, He has special grace and favor ready to be released upon you. You are beloved as much as the perfect Beloved Son. In Jesus, through His blood, we have the forgiveness of our trespasses, according to the riches of His grace (read Ephesians 1:4-7). Just come. If you are thirsty and hungry for God's righteousness, Jesus can satisfy you today.

God's Gracious Forgiveness

There is a story that illustrates what forgiveness is all about. In a faraway kingdom, justice had to be served over a terrible criminal. He had committed the worst of all the crimes. However, a compassionate priest tried to give the criminal a second chance. The religious man asks the king of that kingdom to reconsider the death punishment already scheduled for the criminal. As a righteous leader, the king could not allow that evil man to go unpunished. However, he listened to the priest's plea and said, "The law of our kingdom does not allow criminals to live. However, I will consider your request. The only requirement is that the man shows humble repentance."

"But your majesty..." the priest replied, "How would you know if the man is grieved over his sins?" The wise king said, "Give me your priestly clothes, and I will pay the criminal a visit disguised as you. If the man pleas in repentance for himself before God, I will reconsider his penalty and save him from death."

As the king arrived in prison, the criminal rapidly shouted, "You again, useless priest. I already told you it is unfair that I am being condemned. Yes, sure, I committed a crime, but I could quickly fix that. Besides, what else would you tell me about this merciful God if I told you already that I don't believe in Him? Get out of here. I don't need any help. I already have planned my escape from this prison."

The king left the prison with sorrow. He ordered the guards to reinforce the prison and prepare the prisoner for execution. At the moment of his death punishment, the priest comes to the criminal and reveals the intentions of the king to save him. With the gallows arranged with the prisoner tied on it, the executioner ordered the criminal to say his last words. He said, "I know my crimes. But today, I deserve death not because of them. But because I rejected forgiveness freely given to me."

> [Jesus] is the propitiation for our sins, and not for ours only but also for the sins of the whole world. (1 John 2:2)

> [justification is by] his grace as a gift, through the redemption that is in Christ Jesus, whom God put forward as a propitiation by his blood, to be received by faith. This was to show God's righteousness, because in his divine forbearance, he had passed over former sins. It was to show his righteousness at the present time, so that he might be just and the justifier of the one who has faith in Jesus. (Romans 3:24-26)

Bibliography

Geisler, N.L. and F. Turek, *I don't have enough faith to be an atheist.* Kindle ed. 2021, Wheaton, IL: Crossway Books.

Gilbert, G.D., *What Is The Gospel?* Kindle ed. 2010, Wheaton, IL: Crossway.

Guillen, M., *Believing Is Seeing: A Physicist Explains How Science Shattered His Atheism and Revealed the Necessity of Faith.* Kindle ed. 2021, Carol Stream, IL: Tyndale.

2.
GRACE AND TRUTH

There is no good news until you understand the dire truth about where humanity really is. God only brings the bad news to lead us into the gospel. God would never leave us to the mercy of our own solution. That is why Jesus came with grace and truth.

> *And the Word became flesh and dwelt among us, and we have seen his glory, glory as of the only Son from the Father, full of grace and truth. (John 1:14)*

It is clear to me that full grace walks together with the full truth. Many are still believing in lies because they simply opt to. But you recognize there is a God. Knowing God exists helps you come to terms with your reality. Now you live in a world as if it is worth living in. Beauty and love have a purpose, and people have intrinsic dignity. The grace of life comes only when one accepts the truth that God is here. Ignoring the source of His blessings is deceiving.[1]

---

[1] Timothy Keller, *The Reason for God: Belief in an Age of Scepticism* (London, England: Hodder & Stoughton, 2009). 157-158.

The Father of Lies

Here it is important to recognize who could be behind that deceiving schemes to hide the truth from us. Jesus reveals that the devil is the father of lies and that there is no truth in him.

> [...] the devil [...] was a murderer from the beginning, and does not stand in the truth, because there is no truth in him. When he lies, he speaks out of his own character, for he is a liar and the father of lies. (John 8:44)

Knowing the truth is the only way out of the devil's deceiving enticement. But why would he let that happen? Therefore, it is not by chance that you may be experiencing some resistance to reading this book. Because when you know the truth, the truth sets you free. The truth is the word of Christ. When we learn His words, we receive freedom. (John 8:32 and 36). If needed, the devil would even "disguises himself as an angel of light" when in reality he is pure darkness. (2 Corinthians 11:14). His number one goal is to make mankind not know the truth.

> [...] the god of this world [the devil] has blinded the minds of the unbelievers, to keep them from seeing the light of the gospel of the glory of Christ, who is the image of God. (2 Corinthians 4:4)

There are classic lies that the devil uses to keep someone blind. That is what we will reveal here.

Lie #1: "God does not exist."

We explained in the first chapter that God has expressed Himself in so many ways, but maybe that is the lie holding your faith back. If one falls into that trap, he should start to question many things, like

"Where does this certain that God does not exist come from?", "Can I deny the evidence of a creator displayed in the universe?" But above all, "Why am I willing to have faith in a non-God universe if it is not only to keep my conscience free from accountability?" Someone said wisely, "The unquestionable proof of water's existence is that every creature needs it."

The truth: "God does exist and is all-powerful and loving toward us."

> *[...] "I AM WHO I AM." (Exodus 3:14)*

> *"I am the Alpha and the Omega," says the Lord God, "who is and who was and who is to come, the Almighty." (Revelation 1:8)*

The devil wants that doubt to resonate in your mind to convince you that life is ultimately meanless. But if one heed the Bible, he will learn the amazing news that God not only exists but loves us and has good plans for us.

> *For I know the plans I have for you, declares the LORD, plans for welfare and not for evil, to give you a future and a hope. Then you will call upon me and come and pray to me, and I will hear you. You will seek me and find me, when you seek me with all your heart. (Jeremiah 29:11-13)*

There is hope even for those willing to ask a "nonexistent God" to help them in their unbelief.[2] One day, a desperate father brought his very disabled son before Jesus. The child's illness caused the boy to

---
[2] William Fay and Linda Evans Sheperd, *Share Jesus without Fear* (Nashville, TN: Broadman & Holman, 1999), 91-92.

have seizures and hurt himself. When a loved one has an incurable disorder, we all feel powerless. It was the case for that father. However, Jesus reminded the man.

All things are possible for one who believes. (Mark 9:23).

When the man heard it, he cried and said, "I believe; help my unbelief!" Jesus promptly cured the child, acknowledging the man's sincere plea as an indication of his faith. Anyone can sincerely ask God to help them believe by praying, "God, reveal yourself to me."

Lie #2: "All people are children of God."

Some people are blinded by doubt, and others by incorrect beliefs, which is the devil's work as well. People generally think, "God is the father of everybody. Why should I care to give my life to Jesus and become a believer?" Because, according to the Bible, that is a lie.

The truth: "All people are created by God."

[Jesus] came [but] people did not receive him. But to all who did receive him, who believed in his name, he gave the right to become children of God, who were born, not of blood nor of the will of the flesh nor of the will of man, but of God. (John 1:11-13)

Unless someone believes in Jesus' name, that person remains only a creature, not a son or daughter of God. To be a child of God, you must receive Jesus and believe in His name. That has many implications. Because while one is still only part of the creation, he would still be subjected to the fate of all the misfortunes of this world.

> *For if while we were enemies we were reconciled to God by the death of his Son, much more, now that we are reconciled, shall we be saved by his life. (Romans 5:10)*

Lie #3: "When you die, it's all over anyways."

Jesus spoke about eternal life and eternal punishment (Matthew 25:46 and 2 Thessalonians 1:9). Physical death is not the end of existence. Deep down in our souls, every time we experience grief for the loss of a loved one, we are reminded that life extends beyond this earthly reality. If the enemy of our souls persuades us that there is no afterlife, he will have won.

The truth: "Repentance of sins, leading to trust in Christ, freely gives us eternal life."

> *For the wages of sin is death, but the free gift of God is eternal life in Christ Jesus our Lord. (Romans 6:23)*

It is pointless to deny that death is not the end. The universal fear of death proves my point. If death is only the end, why fear it? Subconsciously, we know we will face God's judgment, so we must accept grace now.

> *Whoever believes in him is not condemned, but whoever does not believe is condemned already, because he has not believed in the name of the only Son of God. (John 3:18)*

A consequence of believing in the lie that "death is the ultimate end" is dulling the issue of wrongdoings before God and others. It pulls other deceiving lies, such as, "Sin is an invention of old and religious folks to limit freedom. Enjoy yourself while you have the chance." But once again, our conscience can't deny that we need God's forgiveness.

> *If we confess our sins, he is faithful and just to forgive us our sins and to cleanse us from all unrighteousness. If we say we have not sinned, we make him a liar, and his word is not in us. (1 John 1:9-10)*

Because of God's grace, we repent and turn from our sins to freely receive His righteousness. That is what gives us eternal life.

Lie #4: "All roads lead to God."

Bethel, a remote city on the western coast of Alaska, is accessed via boat by airplane. There are no roads leading to Bethel—except one. In January, locals cheer on their favorite mushers (sled dog racing) at the three-hundred-mile race from Bethel to the closest city of Aniak. It is that snow-packed path used by dog sleds that is the only road to Bethel. It would be a lie to say that all roads lead to Bethel, for there is only one road that goes there and can be recognized only by the dog racers.[3]

The truth: "Jesus is the only way to God."

> *Jesus said to him, "I am the way, and the truth, and the life. No one comes to the Father except through me. (John 14:6)*

Many people see religion, charity, self-improvement, goodwill, and even "faith in faith" as steps on the imaginary ladder toward reaching heaven. However, believing in this lie leads to eternal death, not God. According to God's word, there is only one true way to

---

[3] "Do All Roads Lead to God?," *Gotquestions.org*, last modified November 24, 2020, accessed July 15, 2023, https://www.gotquestions.org/do-all-roads-lead-to-God.html.

salvation. Everything else is, in reality, a "rail train track" leading to perdition.

> *For by grace you have been saved through faith. And this is not your own doing; it is the gift of God, not a result of works, so that no one may boast. (Ephesians 2:8-9)*

Lie #5: "You have to be good before making a decision for Christ."

If, in one way, some people think they are capable of being all good by themselves, while others believe that they must become a perfect person before coming to Christ. If someone thinks he is good enough or that he must improve himself before coming to Christ, they are both relying on their worthiness before God. That is a lie.

The truth: "Come as you are, and God will change your life."

> *[God] saved us, not because of works done by us in righteousness, but according to his own mercy, by the washing of regeneration and renewal of the Holy Spirit, whom he poured out on us richly through Jesus Christ our Savior, so that being justified by his grace we might become heirs according to the hope of eternal life. (Titus 3:5-7)*

It is important to remember that you are accepted just as you are and that God has the power to transform you from the inside out by His Spirit. Maybe you think God would never accept you because of your past. You consider the terrible things you involved yourself in, and the lying voice of the accuser is holding you away from God. But there is good news for you.

*"**Come now**, let us reason together, says the LORD:
though your sins are like scarlet,
they shall be as white as snow;
though they are red like crimson,
they shall become like wool. (Isaiah 1:18)*

[...] his glorious grace, [...] has blessed us in the Beloved. In him we have redemption through his blood, the forgiveness of our trespasses, according to the riches of his grace, which he lavished upon us [...] (Ephesians 1:6-8)

Come to me, all who labor and are heavy laden, and I will give you rest. (Matthew 11:28)

You may be thinking we are talking about religion here. However, in the next chapter, you will learn that it is not about rituals but about a relationship. It is not about religion. It is about grace.

Bibliography

Fay, William, and Linda Evans Sheperd. *Share Jesus without Fear.* Nashville, TN: Broadman & Holman, 1999.

Keller, Timothy. *The Reason for God: Belief in an Age of Scepticism.* London, England: Hodder & Stoughton, 2009.

"Do All Roads Lead to God?" *Gotquestions.org.* Last modified November 24, 2020. https://www.gotquestions.org/do-all-roads-lead-to-God.html.

GRACE AND PEACE

3.
GRACE, NOT RELIGION

Have you ever wondered why there are so many religions around the world? It seems everyone is running around, anxiously searching for the truth. There are various reasons why humanity is drawn towards chasing after religion. One primary reason is that every human being has the inner desire for a transcendent life. Scientists and anthropologists already agree with multiple types of quotient of intelligence. The famous and well-known IQ and the recently discovered Emotional Intelligence Quotient (EQ)[1]. However, scholars now speak of Spiritual Intelligence because of the universal human spiritual search experience.[2] As controversial as it sounds, humans are essentially spiritual beings. Even those that claim they don't believe in God are stronger "believers" of that atheistic "belief."

Spirituality comes from man's attempts to understand how they can continue their existence after death, knowing that their time on Earth is limited. It is an attempt to find a meaningful purpose. Beyond that, they will do whatever it takes to earn their way into the gates of

---

[1] Daniel Goleman, *Emotional Intelligence: Why It Can Matter More than IQ*, 1st ed. (New York, NY: Random House Publishing Group, 2020).

[2] Guillen, *Believing Is Seeing*, 45.

eternal life. It is the fear of the unknown which produced many religions.

I dare to affirm that all religions can be divided into two groups. Every religion, except Christianity, is in my left hand. Mormonism, Buddhism, Hinduism, Judaism, and any other "ism." Christianity is in my right hand. Everyone on my left hand makes two distinct claims: (a) Jesus is not God, or He is not the only God. He may be a great prophet, teacher, or good man, but not the Savior God; and (b) If you do enough good works through your efforts, such as radical religious acts, diet, or good deeds, you can receive some form of salvation but that is not what we find in the truth of the Christian faith. Therefore, only one is correct. Opposite claims cannot possibly be true.[3]

Called for Relationship, Not for Religion

The teachings of Christ differ from religion. Jesus did not teach a "way" to salvation. He said, "I am the way." (John 14:7). Accepting that "way" is the "only way" to have eternal life. There is no annihilation (like atheism thinks). You either have eternal life, or you will be eternal damned. In all religions, the basis for obtaining salvation is founded on merit.

The word merit implies that someone can earn their way to Heaven. This concept is based upon a person's "good deeds." That describes what religions around the world are attempting to do. It is the belief that God will accept their sacrifices, prayers, fasting, offerings, etc. For them, those doings will be able to atone for their sin.

Believing that we can bribe God or persuade Him to forgive us for our sins based upon our deeds demonstrates that we

---

[3] William Fay and Linda Evans Sheperd, *Share Jesus without Fear* (Nashville, TN: Broadman & Holman, 1999), 176.

misunderstand the severity of our sins before a holy and just God. Trivializing our sin is offensive and insulting to His character. We are powerless within ourselves to please God and atone for our sins. Realize that apart from the saving grace of our Lord, we are not good people. We humbly concluded what the Bible says.

> *[our] heart is deceitful above all things, And desperately wicked; Who can know it? (Jeremiah 17:9 - NKJV).*

How Can We Be Saved?

The Bible teaches that there is only one way to be saved. Salvation comes through repentance of sin and trusting alone in the Savior, Jesus Christ. In other words, you realize how "desperately wicked" you are. After that, you ask for salvation, totally aware of your unworthiness to receive anything. And God, in Christ Jesus, saves you by His grace.

> *Truly, truly, I say to you, whoever hears my word and believes Him who sent me has eternal life. He does not come into judgment, but has passed from death to life. (John 5:24)*

Salvation is a matter of belief. It is not a matter of works but solely based on faith in God's only begotten Son, Jesus Christ. In that sense, Christianity can not be included in the multifold layers of religious options. In essence, in Christianity, it is not humanity trying their way to God, but it is God coming after mankind.

False religious teachers claim that we must strive and "earn" our salvation. However, regardless of one's personal sacrifices, based upon our works, none will be justified before a holy and perfect Judge.

God [saves] you by his grace when you [believe]. And you can't take credit for this; it is a gift from God. Salvation is not a reward for the good things we have done, so none of us can boast about it. (Ephesians 2:8-9 - NLT)

It is not "through works" that we are saved, but rather "through Whom" we are saved. The gift of grace is to experience Jesus Himself.

Amazing Grace, how sweet the sound
That saved a wretch like me
I once was lost, but now am found
I was blind but now I see

Not Only Mercy but Grace

The grace of God is truly more precious than we can imagine. To receive mercy is to be pardoned. It means not receiving the punishment that you deserve. However, grace goes far beyond mercy. To receive grace means to receive all that Jesus deserves without any merit. Grace is always unearned and unmerited. The justification that God gives us is by grace through faith. God gave us His only Son when we deserved His wrath.

We can receive grace freely, but grace was not free. Grace had a price. Yet, it is not a price we could have ever paid ourselves. Grace costs far beyond all the gold, diamonds, and precious stones found on the Earth. Even with all the riches of the world, one could not come near to reaching even a fraction of one percent of what it costs to obtain the grace of God. Grace cost the Father everything; it cost Jesus. The blood of Jesus was the price justice demanded. His blood is the ransom for our freedom (1 Peter 1:18-19). That was the price of redeeming humanity and restoring the divine relationship.

There was absolutely no other substitute. Our penalty for sin was not only the physical death sentence but eternal punishment. In order to fulfill proper reparation, Jesus needed to die the horrific death we deserved. We must understand that Jesus not only endured indescribable physical pain but also took upon Himself the spiritual curses of sin. I pray for you now,

> *Precious Holy Spirit, open our eyes to see precisely what took place on the Cross of Calvary.*

The Problem of Religion

Religion, like the devil, also can blind a person to their real need for grace. That is what Jesus was trying to explain with this story.

> *Two individuals visited a holy site to offer their prayers. One was a devoted religious person, and the other was a despised sinner. The religious one stood by himself and prayed this prayer: "I thank you, God, that I am not like other people—cheaters, sinners, adulterers. I'm certainly not like that transgressor! I fast twice a week, and I give you a tenth of my income."*
>
> *But the repentant sinner kept his distance, not daring to look upward even while he prayed. To express his anguish, he pounded his chest and prayed, "O God, be merciful to me, for I am a sinner."*
>
> *I tell you, the sinner, not the religious one, returned home justified before God. For those who exalt themselves will*

be humbled, and those who humble themselves will be exalted. (Luke18:9-14 - author's paraphrased)

Of all people to whom Jesus spoke, the only group He repeatedly rebuked was the religious one. Why? Because besides not having basic self-awareness, they are quick to condemn others. Religion does not bring people to God. It actually hinders people. At another moment, Jesus met a wealthy young man. He also was very religious. Here, I will paraphrase the story in Matthew 19:16-22.

A young man's approached Jesus with a religious question: "What can I do to save myself? What good am I supposed to do to have eternal life?" Jesus tried to explain to the young man, "First of all, there is no one that is good enough to do good enough to achieve eternal life. But since you can't see that, let me remind you of the Ten Commandments." The young man arrogantly replied, "All these I have kept. What do I still lack?" (Can you notice his blindness? How could that young man not see himself as a wicked sinner? Religion makes that. It closes our eyes to the grace of God because it creates a false sense of merit where, in reality, there is none.)

Back to the story. Jesus, with His particular loving and compassionate looking, said to the young man, "Only perfect people enter heaven. You think you are, but you are not perfect. You lack one thing." (If we are honest with ourselves, we will confess we lack everything, not one thing only. But Jesus was trying to make a point here. To show that religiosity is never enough. Only His grace can save us.)

The greedy young man wondered, "What do I lack?" Jesus said, "Go, sell all that you have and give to the poor." Disheartened by the saying, he went away sorrowful. The religious man left, choosing to keep trying to be perfect without clearly listening to the whole invitation that Jesus said, "Instead of you trying, you can always come and follow me." You can also read this story in Mark 10:17-30.

Grace Transforms While Religion Condemns

Every religion has a set of rules and rituals—a law. People are so used to relating Christianity with religion that some don't even join a church event out of concern with dress code standards. That is because the law is the center of a religious's life. It is true that God gave the law on tablets of stone in the Old Testament. But now, in the New Testament, a New Covenant would be written in our hearts (Hebrews 8:10). Christianity is not legalism.

In some Middle Eastern countries, it is a crime to sell or consume alcohol.[4] Anyone that struggles with alcoholism can be placed in jail or even physically punished. A person with a religious mentality might be happy to think that this legal system is from God. What a mistake. Fear of punishment by the religious law would never change people.

What a difference compared with the grace of God. His grace does not give us a law forbidding us to be sinners, but He transforms us completely, changing our nature. Grace does not give a law. It gives us a new birth. This is the good news of Jesus. Only grace has the power to change man from within (2 Corinthians 5:17).

Religious people, with their "holier-than-thou" attitude, trust their obedience to rituals. They soon think that people will fall into sin if there are no restrictions. But grace changes the believer's nature. We don't murder or commit adultery because grace makes us a new creation, not because of fear of punishment.

---

[4] "Iran: Man Executed for Drinking Alcohol," *Amnesty International*, last modified July 10, 2020, accessed July 14, 2023, https://www.amnesty.org/en/latest/news/2020/07/iran-man-executed-for-drinking-alcohol/.

For Christ is the end of the law for righteousness to everyone who believes. (Romans 10:4)

Besides, once someone puts their faith in Christ, the Spirit of God, the Holy Spirit, will teach them a new way of life. There is no need for rituals or ceremonies. If Christians follow the law of the Spirit, they end up fulfilling the commandments of God. It's not a matter of memorizing norms and rules but of having the living God, through the Holy Spirit residing within us. No one, by himself, can follow the whole law and fully satisfy God's high standards. We need grace every day. It is the Spirit that guides and directs us. We need more grace, not religion.

When the Spirit of truth comes, he will guide you into all the truth, for he will not speak on his own authority, but whatever he hears he will speak, and he will declare to you the things that are to come. (John 16:12-13)

Bibliography

Fay, William, and Linda Evans Sheperd. *Share Jesus without Fear.* Nashville, TN: Broadman & Holman, 1999.

Goleman, Daniel. *Emotional Intelligence: Why It Can Matter More than IQ.* 1st ed. New York, NY: Random House Publishing Group, 2020.

Guillen, Michael. *Believing Is Seeing: A Physicist Explains How Science Shattered His Atheism and Revealed the Necessity of Faith.* Carol Streams, IL: Tyndale Refresh, 2021.

"Iran: Man Executed for Drinking Alcohol." *Amnesty International*. Last modified July 10, 2020. https://www.amnesty.org/en/latest/news/2020/07/iran-man-executed-for-drinking-alcohol/.

GRACE AND PEACE

4.
FROM DARKNESS TO GRACE

When things seem out of control and bad news arrives at an unexpected moment, there is always the chance of God sending you a tiny word. So small that most people don't even think about the power of it. "But." That is the word that can change everything. The accident happened, "but no one was hurt. Your child has a genetic disease. "But" it is easily treatable. You lost your job. "But" you have an excellent idea for a business.

Sadly, sometimes the "but" doesn't come in this fallen world. There are occasions when the terrible news is at the end of the sentence. I remember going through a car accident. Four people were inside the car. "But" we got no scratch. At another moment, my little son hit his head on a piece of wood while playing inside the church building. "But" did not survive. The good "but" never came.

And about the bad news of the sinful condition of all of us? Thank God punishment and judgment are not the end of the story. We were all sinners ready to be condemned. "But" God acted to save us. His action toward us is called grace. There were no merits or worthiness, only God's love working toward each of us.

> ***But*** *God, being rich in mercy, because of the great love with which he loved us, even when we were dead in our trespasses, made us alive together with Christ—by grace you have been saved [...] (Ephesians 2:4-5 emphasis mine)*

God desired to show us the measureless riches of His grace. His kindness is immeasurable toward us in Christ Jesus. The more conscious I am about this love, the more in love I become with God. The word of God makes this outstanding affirmation:

> *For by grace you have been saved through faith. And this is not your own doing; it is the gift of God, not a result of works, so that no one may boast. (Ephesians 2:8-9)*

The Bible is a collection of stories and prophecies to show how God, throughout history, would make that salvation plan available to the whole world. Especially the gospels. They will make it plain that grace is in the person of Jesus.

> *[...] grace and truth came through Jesus Christ. (John 1:17)*

The gospels tell us that Jesus is both totally human and totally God. After all, only a fully human, fully divine Son of God could save us. If He were only a holy man, He would save us just like a dead man can save another dead person, that is, no salvation. However, because He is fully God, with no sin, He is able to defeat death for Himself and also for whoever identifies with His work through faith.

From Dark to the Kingdom of Light

God planned to deliver us from the "Dark Valley." In that terrible place, everything is darkness. We were dead regarding the things of God. Incapable of hearing or understanding spiritual things. People in that place think they are free, but they only follow, like marionette string puppets, what is the next trend. There is no selfless conscience. When one thinks of the divine, it is to mock or rebel against it. The lower impulses of sinful nature are in command. God's righteous wrath is reserved for that people. (Ephesians 2:1-3).

I was a teacher for years, and I remember when we needed to use chalkboards. A dark board written with white chalk. Sometimes, that is how we understand things. Our dark, sinful condition had to become highly evident, which is why God gave humanity His law. Now, our sins also became transgressions. If things were bad, now it is worst. The dark reality is revealed darker.

The people in "Dark Valley" lost their memory of what it even means the light. That is why, by nature, a person will never come to Jesus simply because he does not want God. Humanity is fundamentally at enmity with the things of God. There is no affection for the truth. Satan is a case in point. Satan knows the truth, but he hates the truth. We were like that by nature. Also, we must consider that the master of lies will never allow his slaves to be free so quickly. Consider what Jesus said,

> [...] *you will know the truth, and the truth will set you free. John 8:32*

We Need Jesus

The unbelieving world does not need education. If that were the case, God would have sent an intelligent teacher. The world does not need entertainment, or God would have sent a comedian. We did not need only emotional comfort. For that, God could send a therapist. But we were lost in our sins and transpasses. Incapable of seeing the light. We were alienated from God. We need a deliverer. That is why God sent the savior, the light of the world, Jesus Christ, His Son. The Bible says,

> *In him was life, and the life was the light of men. The light shines in the darkness, and the darkness has not overcome it. (John 1:4-5)*

Without Christ, we could never be delivered from the "domain of darkness." Why? Because we are not sinners because we sin; we sin because we are sinners. It is humanity's radical corruption that prevents them from believing.[1] Since the fall, human nature has been corrupt. We are born with a sinful nature. Our acts of sin flow out of this corrupted nature.

When you watch the daily news, you assume something might be off with humanity. Things are going from bad to worst. There are clashes of opinions that turn into conspiracies and self-centeredness. Political disputes turn into wars. Violence grows more and more inside homes. Just look at what happened with the false world's unity after the Pandemic. We are on the verge of another world war. Why? Because the world lies under the power of the lord of lies and deceit.

Besides, the "darkness emperor," the enemy of our souls, the devil, had a bond with us. We were his slaves. He would never let us go without payment. The Bible called this payment "propitiation." When the price of deliverance is paid, and the slave is set free, the transaction is called "redemption." The ruler of the domain of

---
[1] Sproul, R. C. *What Is Reformed Theology?*, Baker Books, 2016, 137.

darkness required the highest price before giving humanity a chance. Someone else had to pay the fee. Christ Jesus became our propitiation, the cost required for our deliverance.

> *He is the propitiation for our sins, and not for ours only but also for the sins of the whole world. (1 John 2:2)*

While we were dead in our trespasses and our stubbornness of ourselves, God breathed life inside of our hearts to believe in Him and receive His forgiveness of all our sins. This breath of life has been given to us since creation. Why would you not take a deep breath right now? Seriously. Do it now. If you can, say aloud, "Thank you, Father, for your salvation available for me."

God did not only that, but He also offered redemption—the cancellation of spiritual debts. Now, Satan, the accuser, has no more rights. In Christ, God is offering us freedom from all conscience of guilt because by faith, all record of debt that stood against us with its legal demands is nailed to the cross, and the evil spirits lose all their claim upon the believer (Colossians 2:13-15). However, you must appropriate this gift. It will never be imposed on you. Since "forced freedom is a contradiction."[2]

Remember, Jesus is light. Whoever sees that light and responds to His invitation will be set free from darkness. Your pass to the kingdom of light was bought. You must use it to leave that place of death once and for all.

> *For He has rescued us and has drawn us to Himself from the dominion of darkness, and has transferred us to the kingdom of His beloved Son, in whom we have*

---

[2] Geisler, Norman L. and Frank Turek. *I Don't Have Enough Faith to Be an Atheist.* Kindle ed. Wheaton, IL: Crossway Books, 2021, 399.

redemption because of His sacrifice, resulting in the forgiveness of our sins and the cancellation of sins' penalty. (Colossians 1:13-14 - Amplified Bible)

Bibliography

Sproul, R. C. *What Is Reformed Theology? Understanding the Basics.* Kindle ed.: Baker Books, 2016.

GRACE AND PEACE

5.
TIME FOR GRACE

After reading this book, you must come to the following conclusions:

- God loves you deeply. His limitless love was displayed by His creation and by sending His son for us.
- However, we have sinned. Humanity is powerless to fix and save itself, neither by religion nor good works.
- Therefore, Christ had to die for us as humanity's perfect substitute. In His perfect work, Jesus defeated death by resurrecting from the dead.
- Finally, once one understands that, he must respond by trusting God's plan of salvation. Let's respond to some questions regarding your conclusion.

If you did not come to those conclusions yet, please answer with honest words in the following survey.

Survey

Do you have any spiritual views or beliefs? What is it?

- Answer:

Write, with all honesty, what you think about Jesus Christ.

- Answer:

In your spiritual view, is there a place such as heaven or hell?

- Answer:

Where do you think you'd go after you die? Why?

- Answer:

In the following lines, I would like to ask you to read, preferably aloud, some Bible passages. Would you do that? Let's go.

The Gospel Is the Power of God

The word of God, the message of the gospel, has power. I know it sounds strange to some people, but even for those that are not driven by spiritual matters, when they read aloud the Scripture, a new fresh air comes to them. We hope that this happens to you as you read the following verses.

Bible passage #1

for all have sinned and fall short of the glory of God. (Romans 3:23)

Think a little about what you just read. What is your conclusion if this is true? Let's move to the next one.

Bible passage #2

For the wages of sin is death, but the free gift of God is eternal life in Christ Jesus our Lord. (Romans 6:23)

I want you to consider that there is no "s" in the word "sin." That has some explanations (for example, it speaks of the unfixable sinful nature, innate sin), but let's stay with the basics. It means that God, to be the perfect righteous judge, would have to sentence even if there is only one sin. The word "death" here means "eternal death" or its equivalent, that is, "hell."

Bible passage #3

Jesus [said], "Truly, truly, I say to you, unless one is born again he cannot see the kingdom of God." (John 3:3)

If you read correctly, the only way to heaven, according to Jesus, is to be born again. There is no work, religiosity or deeds that would make a person improved enough for heaven or blessings. One must be born again.

Bible passage #4

[Jesus] came [...] and [...] people did not receive him. But to all who did receive him, who believed in his name, he gave the right to become children of God, who were born, not of blood nor of the will of the flesh nor of the will of man, but of God. (John 1:11-13)

The new birth is not something you do to yourself. You must be begotten, generated from the God the Father. Our part is "receive

Him." This receiving is not only mental assent. It must be expressed with a response.

Bible passage #5

> *because, if you confess with your mouth that Jesus is Lord and believe in your heart that God raised him from the dead, you will be saved. For with the heart one believes and is justified, and with the mouth one confesses and is saved. For the Scripture says, "Everyone who believes in him will not be put to shame." (Romans 10:9-11)*

That's it. Now you have to give God an answer. The positive answer would be faith in your heart and confession with your mouth. Once you respond to that grace invitation, the promises of Jesus are amazing. Starting with what we said in the opening of this book. Real peace. Peace with God and peace of Christ in you. Jesus said,

> *[...] my peace I give to you. Not as the world gives do I give to you. Let not your hearts be troubled, neither let them be afraid. (John 14:27)*

The Most Important Five "Yes" of Your Life

- After reading the previous scriptures, do you recognize that you are a sinner? - Romans 3:23

    ( ) Yes

- Do you want forgiveness for your sins right now? – Romans 6:23

    ( ) Yes

- Do you want to be born again? – John 3:3

    ( ) Yes

- Do you believe in your heart that Jesus died on the cross for you and rose again to give you eternal life? – Romans 10:9-11

    ( )Yes

- Are you willing to surrender your life to Jesus Christ by inviting Him into your heart right now?

    ( )Yes

These five "yes" are all you need to make the most important prayer of your life. Would you, with all your heart and mind, also, if possible, repeat aloud the following prayer?

The most important prayer

Heavenly Father, I have sinned against you. I want forgiveness for all my sins.

I believe that Jesus is your Son. I believe that He died on the cross for me. I believe that He rose again to give me eternal life.

Father God, I give you my life. You can do whatever you wish with me. I am yours.

I want Jesus to come into my life.

I ask the Holy Spirit to fill my heart.

I believe and confess Jesus as my Lord and Savior.

This I pray, in Jesus' name. Amen.

GRACE AND PEACE

APPENDIX. STEPS OF GRACE

Now that you are saved, God has so much in store waiting for you.

Step #1

The first thing I want you to do is to tell someone about your decision. Yes, you heard me right. That is your first step as a new disciple of Christ. There is nothing to be afraid of. When we do that, our faith gets stronger.

A great way to give witness to your faith in Christ is simply accepting the water of baptism. Jesus said,

> *"Whoever believes and is baptized will be saved [...]" (Mark 16:16).*

One of the most incredible things that happen with the new believer in Christ is that their identity is completely changed. Your old story is over. The new life of God has come.

> *Therefore, if anyone is in Christ, he is a new creation. The old has passed away; behold, the new has come. (2 Corinthians 5:17)*

Not only that. You also are chosen to proclaim your new story to those that never heard about that amazing grace and peace you have received.

> *But you are a chosen race, a royal priesthood, a holy nation, a people for his own possession, that you may proclaim the excellencies of him who called you out of darkness into his marvelous light. Once you were not a people, but now you are God's people; once you had not received mercy, but now you have received mercy. (1 Peter 2:9-10) (Read also Revelation 1:5- 6)*

Step #2

Your second step is to be connected with a small group. We like to call them LifeGroups. We call them LifeGroups because they are meant to be a life-giving and life-sharing experience where every believer can use their talents and bless one another. Small groups are all about sharing stories, and reaching out to a broken world with the love of Jesus is what. For us, as a church movement, it's all about building a relationship with Jesus, with one another, and reaching the world from house to house, city to city, nation to nation.[1]

You and I exist to make overcoming disciples who make disciples through LifeGroups that multiply.

> *[the disciples of Christ] continuing daily with one accord in the temple, and breaking bread from **house to house**, they ate their food with gladness and simplicity of heart, praising God and having favor with all the people. And*

---

[1] Larry Kreider, *House to House, by Nurturing Thrive-Inducing Small Groups and House Churches in the Twenty-First Century* (Shippensburg, PA: House to House Publications, 2008), 59.

the Lord added to the church daily those who were being saved. (Acts 2:46-47 - NKJV)

Each one of us is meant to live a transcendent life beyond our personal and selfish desires. God is calling us to live a purpose-driven life, and that is only possible when we change the "I," "me," and "mine" for "we," "us," and "our." Christianity was designed to live in the context of "one another." There are various Bible instructions on that matter. Please take a look at some of them.

Love one another (John 13:34). Honor one another above yourselves (Romans 12:10). Build up one another (Romans 14:19; 1 Thessalonians 5:11). Accept one another (Romans 15:7). Care for one another (1 Corinthians 12:25). Serve one another (Galatians 5:13). Forgive one another (Ephesians 4:2, 32; Colossians 3:13). Consider others better than yourselves (Philippians 2:3). Look to the interests of one another (Philippians 2:4).

Therefore, a believer should never embrace the idea that the walking of faith is a lone journey. That is one of the most common traps on your way to spiritual growth.

Step #3

The third step is one of the most essential steps you must take. As we learned here, the message of Jesus, the gospel, is not a set of doctrines and concepts. The gospel is a transformative experience with the grace and peace of God. To fully get that, consider joining one of our Encounters where you can actually experience the message of the Bible. The gospel is not only meant to be understood but also personally experienced.

For I am not ashamed of the gospel, for it is the power of God for salvation [transformation] to everyone who believes [...] (Romans 1:16)

Step #4

Don't miss the next opportunity to give God worship and praise for what He has done for you. The church service is the place for that. Every Sunday, hundreds of thousands of Christians gather worldwide to celebrate their salvation and encourage one another by offering God worship and their gratitude generosity.

The church service is also a great way to use your gifts. There are so many ways to participate on our Service Flow Team. This team is a group of volunteers that use their talents for various needs. I'm sure you'll love to get part of one of those teams.

Therefore, my beloved brothers, be steadfast, immovable, always abounding in the work of the Lord, knowing that in the Lord your labor is not in vain. (1 Corinthians 15:58)

Step #5

Your final step is to be an overcoming follower of Christ. For that, we developed the Overcomer Track. The track starts with the Baptism course and Vine Experience. We would like to resource you to grow in maturity and prepare you to be a disciple who makes disciples through LifeGroups that multiply. God is calling you to be a leader who can empower others through your gifts being used in our LifeGroups.

His divine power has granted to us all things that pertain to life and godliness, through the knowledge of him who called us to his own glory and excellence, by which he has granted to us his precious and very great promises, so that through them you may become partakers of the divine nature, having escaped from the corruption that is in the world because of sinful desire. For this very reason, make every effort to supplement your faith with virtue, and virtue with knowledge, and knowledge with self-control, and self-control with steadfastness, and steadfastness with godliness, and godliness with brotherly affection, and brotherly affection with love. (2 Peter 1:3-7)

This short booklet is only the beginning of the adventure with God. Are you ready for more grace and peace?

Check our website for more equipping resources.

www.vineSWFL.church

Bibliography

Kreider, Larry. *House to House, by Nurturing Thrive-Inducing Small Groups and House Churches in the Twenty-First Century.* Shippensburg, PA: House to House Publications, 2008.

Made in the USA
Middletown, DE
30 March 2024

52333041R00033